EARTH

The Illustrated Geography of Our World

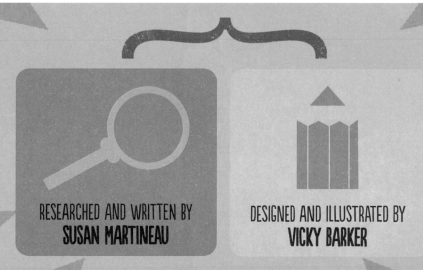

RESEARCHED AND WRITTEN BY
SUSAN MARTINEAU

DESIGNED AND ILLUSTRATED BY
VICKY BARKER

FOR YOUNG READERS

Racehorse for Young Readers

EARTH IN SPACE

There are billions of stars in the Universe. Stars look small, but they are really huge balls of burning gas. Some stars also have massive balls of rock, or planets, circling around them. Planet Earth orbits a star called the Sun. Other planets also orbit the Sun to make a space neighborhood that we call the Solar System.

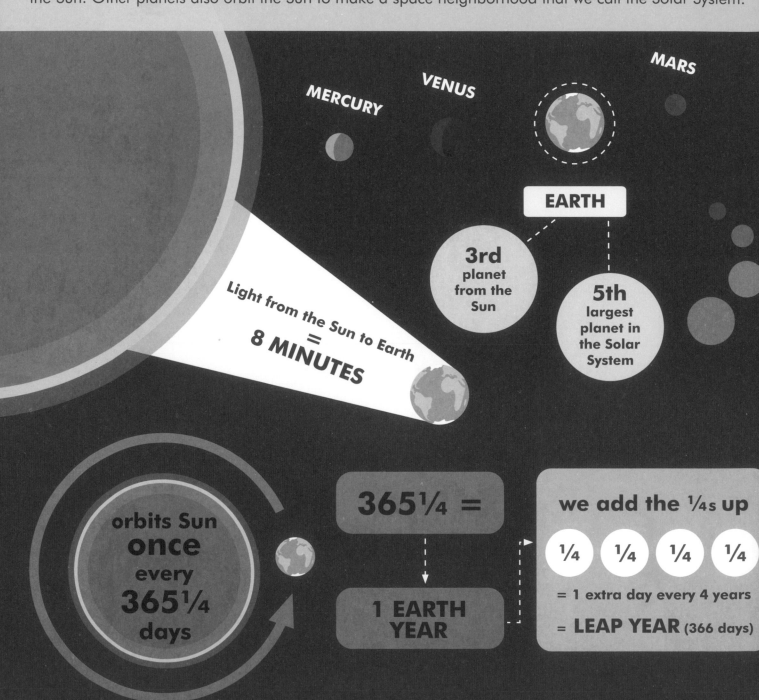

MERCURY

VENUS

MARS

EARTH

3rd planet from the Sun

5th largest planet in the Solar System

Light from the Sun to Earth
=
8 MINUTES

orbits Sun **once** every **365¼** days

365¼ =

1 EARTH YEAR

we add the ¼s up

¼ ¼ ¼ ¼

= 1 extra day every 4 years

= **LEAP YEAR** (366 days)

An **ASTRONOMER** investigates stars, planets, and galaxies. Astronomy is the study of everything in the Universe.

PLUTO   ERIS

JUPITER

SATURN

URANUS

NEPTUNE

Earth has 1 moon

The Moon is getting further away from Earth by about as much as your fingernails grow each year.

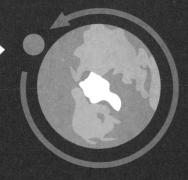

spins on its own axis every 24 hours

DAY

NIGHT

If **33** **MILLION** **PEOPLE** **held hands** around the Earth's waist or **Equator** they would **go right around** the planet.

A LOT OF PEOPLE WOULD BE TREADING WATER!

If EVERYONE in the world joined in...

we would make **200** rings around the Earth.

Planet Earth is not a perfectly round sphere. It's really the shape of a slightly squashed ball. It is a little flatter at the top and the bottom.

NORTH POLE

SOUTH POLE

3

THE ATMOSPHERE

There is a giant blanket of air around Planet Earth. It is called the atmosphere and it is made of different layers. The layer nearest Earth is really important as it keeps us warm and gives us oxygen to breathe. It is also where our weather happens.

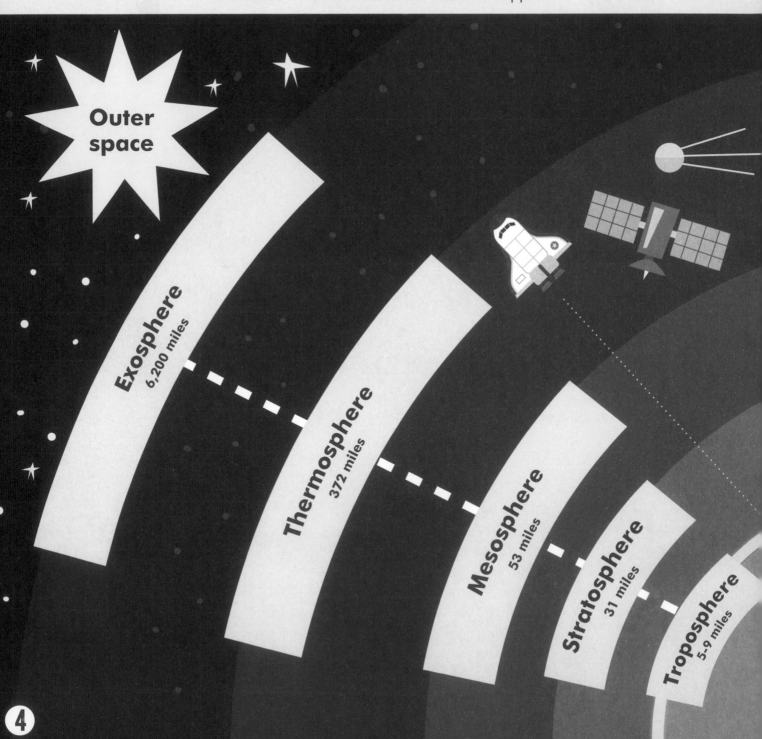

Outer space

Exosphere
6,200 miles

Thermosphere
372 miles

Mesosphere
53 miles

Stratosphere
31 miles

Troposphere
5-9 miles

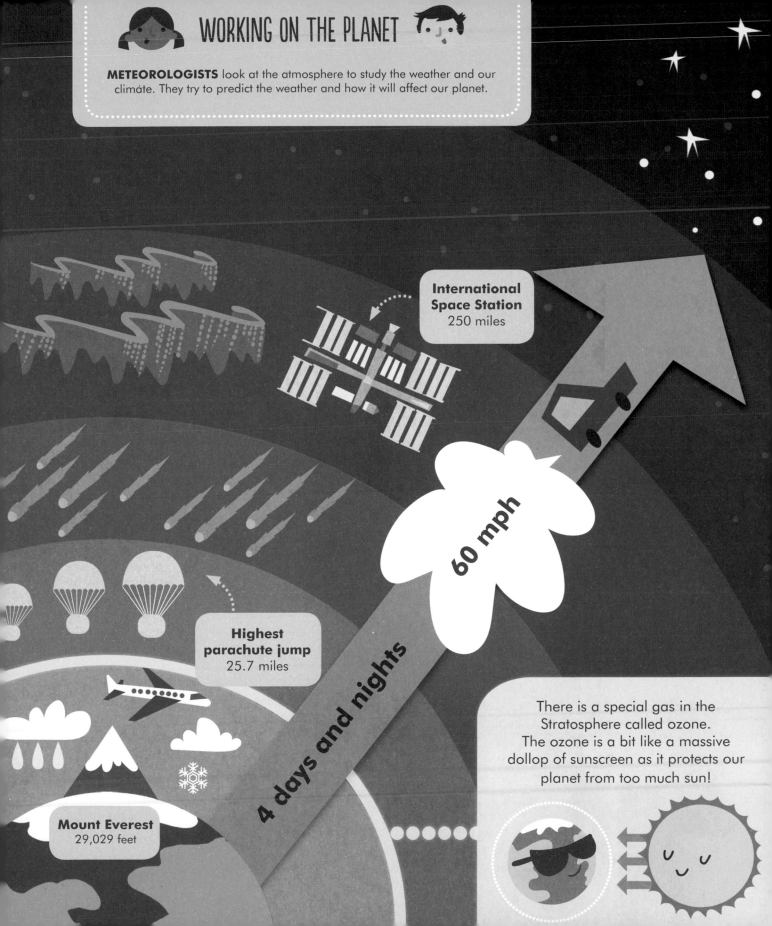

WORKING ON THE PLANET

METEOROLOGISTS look at the atmosphere to study the weather and our climate. They try to predict the weather and how it will affect our planet.

International Space Station
250 miles

60 mph

Highest parachute jump
25.7 miles

4 days and nights

Mount Everest
29,029 feet

There is a special gas in the Stratosphere called ozone. The ozone is a bit like a massive dollop of sunscreen as it protects our planet from too much sun!

JOURNEY TO THE CENTER OF THE EARTH

The Earth under our feet is like a giant onion with four layers. No one has ever travelled to the center of the planet, but scientists think that they know what might be in each layer. They also think that the very center of the Earth is actually a solid ball of metal.

CRUST

about **19 miles thick** on land and about **3 miles thick** at the bottom of the ocean

1

MANTLE

1,800 miles thick

2

Made of hot, molten rock

Made of rocks

3 rock families

IGNEOUS (made from hot, molten rock)

SEDIMENTARY (layers of worn-down rock)

METAMORPHIC (rocks changed by heat and pressure)

Rocks in **CRUST** made of over **2,000 MINERALS**

which include metals like gold and iron and precious stones like diamonds and sapphires.

7.5 miles

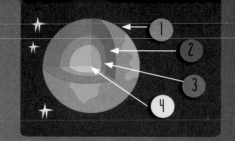

GEOLOGISTS study the solid surface of our planet. They investigate how our planet was first made by looking at the rocks in and on it.

HOTTEST PART
of core is as hot as the Sun
10,800°F

OUTER CORE
1,367 miles thick

3

INNER CORE
radius 758 miles

4

Made of liquid metal

Made of solid metal

It would take me a month at **6 mph...**

... to get to the center of the Earth!

SO HOT and under **SO MUCH PRESSURE** = **LIQUID METAL GOES SOLID**

The deepest hole ever drilled is in Russia and is called the Kola Superdeep Borehole. It took **20 years** to reach a depth of

7.5 miles

before the drill got too hot to carry on!

Inner core rotates (turns) more quickly than the rest of the Earth's layers.

But it takes

1,000

years to do one extra rotation!

MOVING PLATES

The ground you walk on is not as solid as you might think. The surface of the Earth is like a massive jigsaw of pieces or "plates" that move. These plates are under the oceans and seas, too.

Arctic Ocean

North America

Europe

Asia

Atlantic Ocean

Pacific Ocean

Equator

Africa

Pacific Ocean

South America

Indian Ocean

Australia

Atlantic Ocean

Antarctica

Scientific name for plates =

TECTONIC PLATES

Plates make the Earth's continents move from

½ inch

to 4 inches in a year.

Plates are **thinner** under oceans than on land.

SEISMOLOGISTS study earthquakes. They measure the shock waves caused by earthquakes and they try to predict when earthquakes will happen. This can save lives.

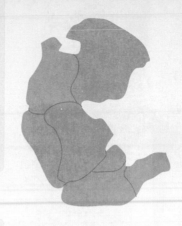

About **270 million** years ago the continents on our planet used to be one giant slab of land. Scientists call this mega-continent **Pangaea.**

Volcanoes

Most of the world's active volcanoes lie where

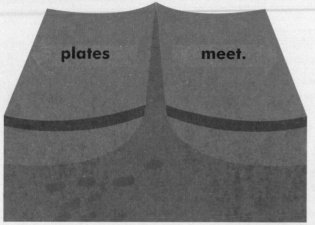

plates   meet.

Earthquakes

happen when plates slip against each other.

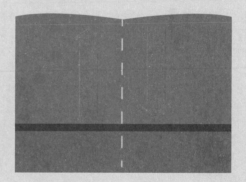

 ACTIVE ➡ could **ERUPT** again!

 Planet Earth has **1,900 ACTIVE** volcanoes.

Tsunamis

big earthquakes under the ocean

gigantic, destructive waves

Earthquake   **Shock wave**   **Tsunami**

 In 2004 a tsunami in the Indian Ocean killed over **230,000** people.

Speed of wave was as fast as a plane

500 mph

THE BLUE PLANET

Water covers more than two thirds of our beautiful planet. If you look at a map of the whole world you ca[n] see that the oceans are really all joined up. If you dip your toes in one ocean you are really dipping them into all the oceans on Earth!

5 MAIN OCEANS
How all the water in the oceans is divided up:

PACIFIC
50.1%

ATLANTIC
23.3%

INDIAN
19.8%

SOUTHERN
OR ANTARCTIC
5.4%

ARCTIC
1.4%

But you would not want to drink this water. It's salty!

Pacific covers ONE THIRD of Earth's surface.

It is **3 x BIGGER** than the **BIGGEST CONTINENT...**

ASIA.

An **OCEANOGRAPHER** explores the oceans from the depths of the sea floor to the surface and everything in between!

Waves are very powerful. The power of a wave crashing on to a beach is **30** times more powerful than the pressure of a human foot. This is how waves can smash rocks into sand!

Pacific Ocean contains

- 0 ft
- 3,275 ft.
- 6,550 ft.
- 9,825 ft.
- 13,100 ft.
- 16,375 ft.
- 19,650 ft.
- 22,925 ft.
- 26,200 ft.
- 29,475 ft.
- 32,750 ft.
- 36,025 ft.

DEEPEST PLACE ON EARTH

Mariana Trench =
36,201 feet

That's over
6.8 miles down!

The highest mountain on Earth would fit in it!

Mount Everest =
29,029 feet

Atlantic covers over **ONE FIFTH** of Earth's surface.

Indian is the **WARMEST** ocean.

Southern is around the SOUTH POLE. STRONGEST WINDS on Earth.

Arctic is around the NORTH POLE. FROZEN for most of the year.

NO LIFE WITHOUT WATER

There would be no life on Planet Earth without water. It fills the oceans and rivers, and it is in the air as water vapor. It is all around us. But did you know that when it rains it is not new water?

2 Water vapo cools an **CONDENSES** It turns bac into tiny drops water and makes cloud

1 Water **EVAPORATES** as the sun heats it. It changes into water vapor and rises up.

How our planet recycles water...

5 Water flows back to the oceans.

WORKING ON THE PLANET

HYDROLOGISTS are scientists who study water. They look at water on the surface of Earth, in the soil, under the ground, and in the atmosphere. They can help us save precious water supplies.

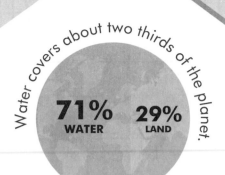

Water covers about two thirds of the planet.

71% WATER **29%** LAND

3

Clouds move inland. Water drops cool down more and fall as rain or snow.

There is not much **FRESH** water on Earth.

97% SALT water

3% FRESH water

Glaciers

Underground

29% **70%**

1% Rivers & lakes

Rain fills rivers and lakes.

4

Rain soaks underground.

There is the same amount of water on Earth today as there was when the dinosaurs roamed the planet.

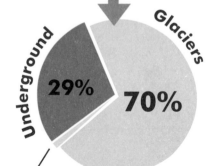

THE BREATHING PLANET

Humans and other animals need a gas called oxygen to breathe. Oxygen in the Earth's atmosphere is made by plants and trees on land, and by tiny plants in the oceans. We need all these plants to make sur we have enough oxygen to stay alive!

2 BILLION YEARS AGO

Oxygen built up in the atmosphere and water of Earth. It turned the sky and the seas blue.

AIR IN ATMOSPHERE

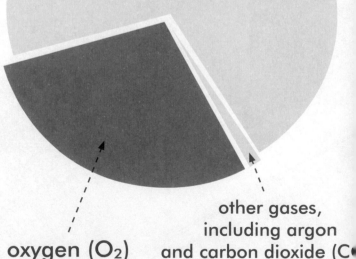

nitrogen
78%

oxygen (O₂)
21%

other gases, including argon and carbon dioxide (C

1%

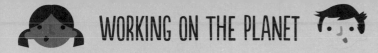

WORKING ON THE PLANET

BOTANISTS are scientists who study everything to do with plants. The more we know about plant life, the better we can protect it.

The higher up into the atmosphere you go

the thinner air gets.

It means there is less oxygen to breathe, too. That is why mountain climbers need to take extra oxygen with them!

LUNGS OF THE WORLD

Photosynthesis
Plants and trees use sunlight, water, and carbon dioxide to make food for themselves.

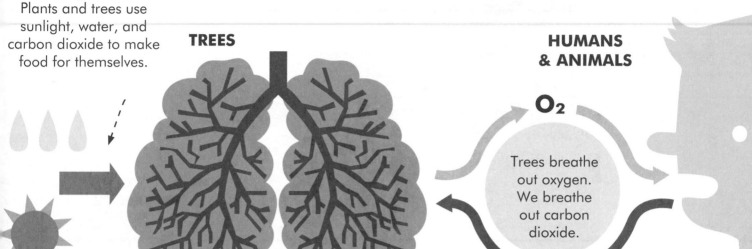

TREES

HUMANS & ANIMALS

O_2

Trees breathe out oxygen. We breathe out carbon dioxide.

CO_2

PERSON needs the oxygen from up to 8 **TREES** to breathe for **1 YEAR.**

Rainforests are so huge...

... they "breathe in" LOTS of carbon dioxide

... and "breathe out" LOTS of oxygen.

RESPIRATION is the scientific name for breathing.

15

CLIMATES OF THE WORLD

The world can be divided into different climate zones. Climate is not the same as weather. The weather can change in just a few hours, but climate takes hundreds, or even millions, of years to change.

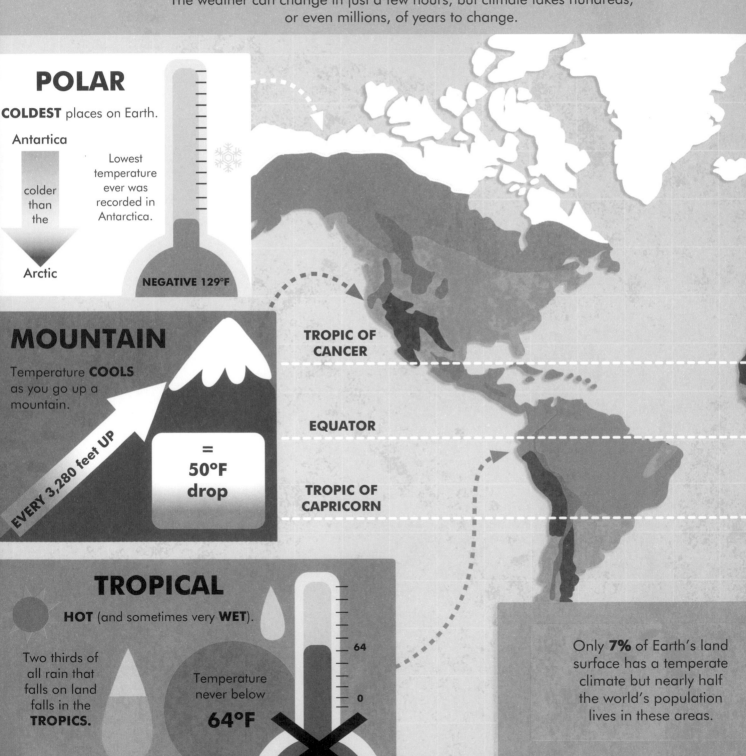

POLAR

COLDEST places on Earth.

Antartica

colder than the

Arctic

Lowest temperature ever was recorded in Antarctica.

NEGATIVE 129°F

MOUNTAIN

Temperature **COOLS** as you go up a mountain.

EVERY 3,280 feet **UP**

=
50°F drop

TROPIC OF CANCER

EQUATOR

TROPIC OF CAPRICORN

TROPICAL

HOT (and sometimes very **WET**).

Two thirds of all rain that falls on land falls in the **TROPICS**.

Temperature never below **64°F**

64

0

Only **7%** of Earth's land surface has a temperate climate but nearly half the world's population lives in these areas.

WORKING ON THE PLANET

CLIMATE SCIENTISTS measure the way the weather changes over a long time. They investigate how much of this is because of what humans are doing on the planet, or if they are changes that would happen anyway.

COLD

FREEZING for up to 6 months every year.

TEMPERATE

NOT TOO HOT/NOT TOO COLD
4 seasons.

DESERT

DRIEST places on Earth.

HOT enough to fry an egg during the day.

COLD enough to freeze water at night.

GREENHOUSE PLANET

Earth's atmosphere is like a greenhouse. It keeps us warm and helps trees and plants to grow. Gases in the atmosphere stop all of the Sun's heat just bouncing off our planet. But our greenhouse is getting too warm because there is too much of one particular greenhouse gas.

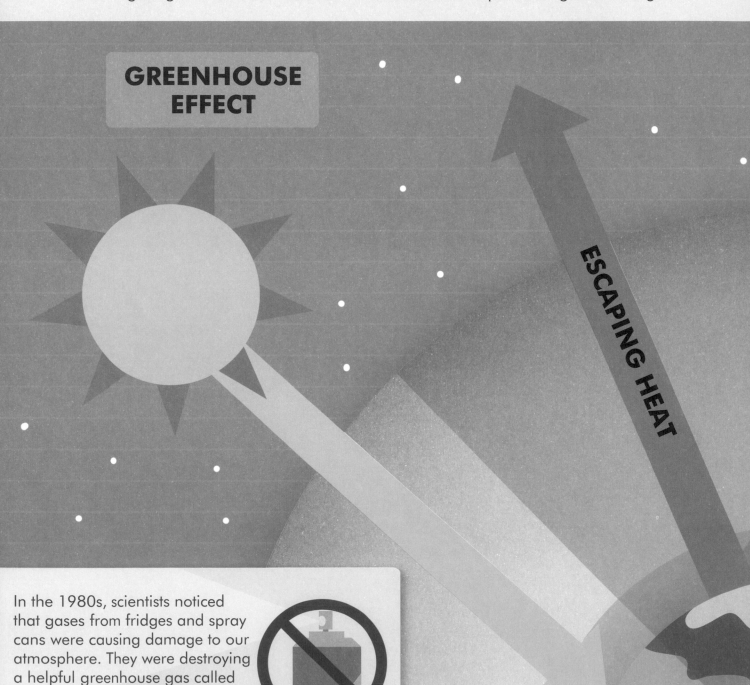

GREENHOUSE EFFECT

ESCAPING HEAT

In the 1980s, scientists noticed that gases from fridges and spray cans were causing damage to our atmosphere. They were destroying a helpful greenhouse gas called ozone. Most countries have now banned these harmful gases.

WORKING ON THE PLANET

ENVIRONMENTAL SCIENTISTS use their scientific knowledge to try and protect our planet from harmful changes. They can advise people on how to look after our beautiful Earth.

Cutting down trees
=

fuel   farmland   roads

trees take in CO_2 but release CO_2 when cut down

methane   water vapor   **CARBON DIOXIDE (CO_2)**

Burning fossil fuels
(coal, oil, gas)
=

electricity   cars   planes

puts lots of CO_2 into atmosphere

greenhouse gases trapping too much of the Sun's heat

TRAPPED HEAT

MORE CARBON DIOXIDE in atmosphere

+

RISE in Earth's **AVERAGE** temperature

=

CHANGES in climate

76% of greenhouse gas emissions are CO_2.

ice caps and glaciers melting

unusual weather

= **FLOODS**

= **AFFECTS CROPS AND ANIMALS**

INTO THE WOODS

Trees are amazing. Some of them can live for thousands of years. Forests cover about one third of the land on Earth. Different types, or species, of trees grow in a forest depending on where that forest is in the world.

Forests are "carbon sinks." They soak up the carbon dioxide that is causing dangerous changes to our planet's climate. This means it is very important to protect our forests as they look after us and our Earth home.

DECIDUOUS FOREST

WHERE:

temperate places

Not too hot, not too cold

LEAVES:

deciduous → fall in autumn

BEST FACTS:

1 oak tree =

250,000 leaves

50,000 acorns

each spring.

WORKING ON THE PLANET

FOREST RANGERS protect forests and all the trees and animals in them. They can spot any damage and take steps to repair forests if needed.

CONIFEROUS FOREST

WHERE:
cold mountains

LEAVES:

 evergreen → don't fall

BEST FACTS:

Longest pine cone	Oldest trees in world
=	=
Sugar Pine **2 feet**	Bristlecone Pines **5,000 years old**

= size of a baby

= age of the pyramids of Egypt

TROPICAL RAINFOREST

WHERE:
hot and rainy places

LEAVES:

big and wide →
absorb lots of carbon dioxide

BEST FACTS:

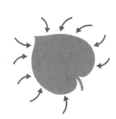

1 hectare (2.5 acres)

100 different tree species

Rain can take up to **10 minutes** to reach the ground.

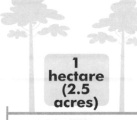

DESERTED EARTH

Deserts are the driest places on Earth. Deserts can be scorching hot, but did you know that deserts can be very cold, too? In fact, Antarctica and the Arctic are polar deserts!

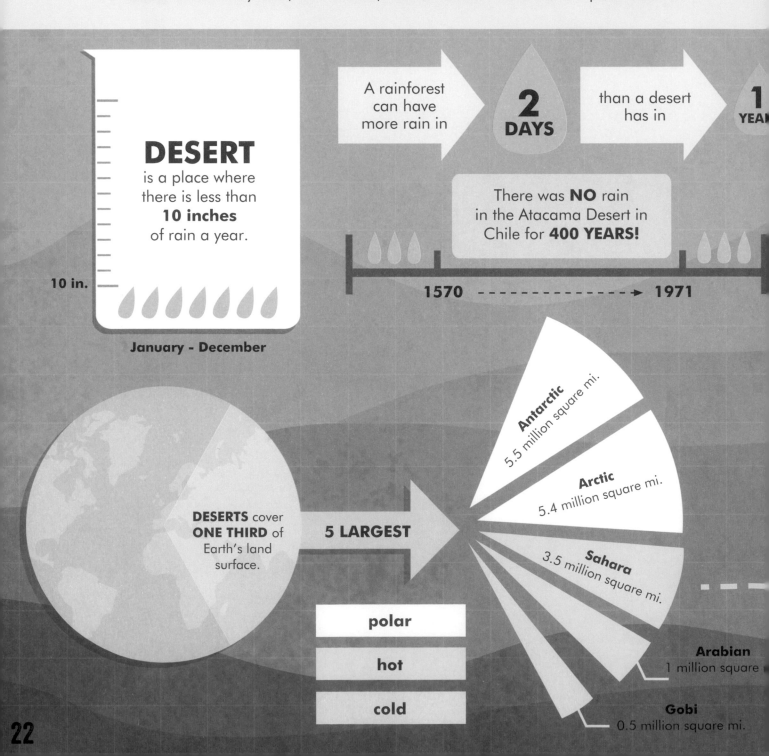

DESERT is a place where there is less than **10 inches** of rain a year.

10 in.

January - December

A rainforest can have more rain in **2 DAYS** than a desert has in **1 YEAR**

There was **NO** rain in the Atacama Desert in Chile for **400 YEARS!**

1570 - - - - - - - - → 1971

DESERTS cover **ONE THIRD** of Earth's land surface.

5 LARGEST

Antarctic 5.5 million square mi.

Arctic 5.4 million square mi.

Sahara 3.5 million square mi.

Arabian 1 million square

Gobi 0.5 million square mi.

polar

hot

cold

22

WORKING ON THE PLANET

An **ECOLOGIST** studies how environments, like deserts, affect the animals and plants living in them. The ecologist looks at the smallest forms of life as well as the bigger "picture" of the environment.

The **Antarctic** and **Arctic** deserts are always cold, but even hot deserts can be cold at night. The boiling hot day temperatures can drop down to freezing.

32°F

"SAHARA" = **"DESERT"** in Arabic

The **Sahara** is bigger than the **USA** and getting **BIGGER** every day.

SANDSTORMS can **BLAST** the paint off a car!

Sahara is

sand

30%

70%

gravel

EARTH WORDS TO KNOW

ACTIVE
An active volcano is one that might erupt. It could throw out lots of hot, melted rock (magma).

ATMOSPHERE
is the air all around Planet Earth. It is made of different layers.

AXIS
The Earth's axis is an imaginary line drawn between the North and South Poles. The Earth tilts slightly on its axis.

BILLION
is a thousand million or 1,000,000,000.

CARBON DIOXIDE (CO_2)
A type of gas in the Earth's atmosphere. It is also the gas we breathe out and that plants and trees breathe in.

CONDENSE
means to change from a gas into a liquid, usually when a gas cools down.

CONTINENT
A very large area of land.

DECIDUOUS
Deciduous trees lose their leaves in autumn and grow new ones in the spring.

ENVIRONMENT
is the air, water, or land that people and animals live in or on.

EQUATOR
is an imaginary line that runs around the middle of the Earth.

EVAPORATE
means to change from a liquid into a gas, usually by heating the liquid.

EVERGREEN
Evergreen trees and plants do not lose their leaves in autumn. They stay green all year.

GALAXY
A huge collection of stars and planets. The Universe contains billions of galaxies.

GLACIER
A huge river of ice that moves very slowly down mountains.

MINERALS
are crystals inside rocks. They are like the "building blocks" of rocks.

MOLTEN
means melted into liquid.

ORBIT
means to circle around something.

OXYGEN (O_2)
A gas in the atmosphere that humans and many living things need to breathe.

OZONE
A gas in the atmosphere that helps to absorb most of the harmful rays of the Sun.

PHOTOSYNTHESIS
is how plants and trees use sunshine, water, and carbon dioxide to make food for themselves.

PRECIPITATION
means water falling as snow, rain, or hail.

PRESSURE
is when something pushes or presses down or against something else.

RADIUS
A straight line from the center to the edge of a circle or sphere.

RESPIRATION
is the scientific name for breathing.

ROTATE
means to make a circle, or rotation, around an axis or center.

SHOCK WAVE
A sudden wave of very high pressure moving through the air, earth, or water. It is caused by earthquakes or explosions.

SPECIES
A group of animals or plants that are similar.

TECTONIC
means to do with the Earth's crust, how it is formed, and how it is still changing.

TEMPERATE
means not too hot and not too cold.

TROPICAL
Tropical areas are just to the north and south of the Equator. They are very hot and wet.

UNIVERSE
The name given to everything that exists in space and time.

WATER VAPOR
is water in the form of a gas. Steam and mist are water vapor.